Digital Outback

Cyberpunk and Culture on the Edge of the Net

Daniel Messer

Digital Outback: Cyberpunk and Culture on the Edge of the Net by Daniel Messer.

To console cowboys
Phreaks and geeks
Hacktivists
Pentesters and pirates
Hackers and crackers

And to those who write the code

Welcome to the Future, Welcome to the Now

I have a hypothesis, but I think there's plenty of evidence to support it. I believe William Gibson stopped writing cyberpunk novels because they're no longer futuristic. If you've read any of his later novels, starting with *Pattern Recognition,* they're set in the future, but only just a little. Pattern Recognition was published in 2003 and, for the most part, everything in it could happen today. One of the biggest reasons I write about and work within the cyberpunk philosophy is because I don't see cyberpunk as being the future.

It's now. Right now.

Look around you. The United States Armed Forces are working on a self-aiming assault rifle guided by computers and GPS. Even more interesting is that these rifles run on Linux, a free and open source operating system for the masses and those masses include the Federal Government. Soldiers coming back from the wars with missing limbs can look into prosthetic limbs that are, quite frankly, the first generation of cybernetic replacements. One looks at these things and wonder how long it will be before they're so good, people voluntarily have limbs replaced with them.

Russian smugglers were recently caught using homemade drones to smuggle cigarettes. Think about that, and you'll quickly realize that if the Russians are doing it so are the Central and South American Cartels. After all, a drone doesn't have to be stealthy, it just has to fly below the radar. Like a drone operator here in America, the pilot can be miles away and in very little danger of getting caught. Meanwhile, DARPA is looking at the military and intelligence implications of the Oculus Rift and what it might be used for in what will no doubt be the next generation of cyber-warfare.

And me, I'm sitting here writing this screed on a laptop that weighs just over a kilogram. It's made of aluminum and connects to a global information network without any wires or cables.

I take it with me everywhere and use it for everything. When I want to listen to music, my phone brings it to me over that information network. I can listen to radio all over the world and learn anything I want… all I need is a connection and some time.

Welcome to the cyberpunk future starting in 4… 3… 2…

Online money making means advertisements and commercials. Granted, ads aren't the only way to generate income online, not in this age of Patreon and Kickstarter. Even so, people need to know about the Patreon, Kickstarter, and GoFundMe campaigns for them to be at all successful and that means advertising the campaign. I speak from experience on this front because, over a year ago, I created a Patreon account for my podcasts and an upcoming YouTube series that I'm working on.

I never wound up using it. Given the nature of my shows, I feel kind of weird taking money for them, even tips. That's my own personal hang-up and we won't get into that right now. I set up the account, populated it with some basic content for an upcoming push, and then I told absolutely no one about it. I've never mentioned it on my shows, and I've never brought it up in a video or an interview. Indeed, this is the first time I've told anyone about it, and I'm not even going to bother doing anything with it now because, frankly, I don't think I have anything worth paying for yet.

Needless to say, it's made precisely zero dollars because I never advertised it.

Want people to contribute to your Patreon? You need to tell them about it. Want people to back your Kickstarter? You need to tell them about it. That means a quick advertising spot or outright commercial on your podcast, video, or whatever. So once again, if you want to make some money online, then you need to advertise.

Moving away from personal podcasts and the equivalent of mom-and-pop online stores, let's move up to social networking and sharing services. I add the word "sharing" in there because more and more of social networking is sharing things, whether it be a quick video on Vine or a photo on Instagram. Live video feeds are trending in popularity as Periscope allows the world to see what you see, right now, as it happens.

* * *

Whether it's sharing photos, audio, video, or a simple link; all of these services have something in common, the people behind them would like to make some money. That's fair and totally expected. While there are a few ways they could go about this, advertising is the path of least resistance. There are other methods, of course. There could be a subscription fee so you can't use the service, or use all of the service, without a monthly payment. The site could try working off donations or a virtual tip jar. Maybe that'd work, but probably not, and services like Twitter, YouTube, Facebook, Google+, Instagram, Vine, Periscope, Snapchat, and Tumblr haven't even tried. Sponsored content allows everyone to play along and they'll have to put up with some ads along the way. Maybe it's a boosted post on Facebook, a sponsored tweet on Twitter, or even a guy on Vine who takes money to make six second commercials.

Think about that. Six second commercials. Compare that to *the five* seconds that YouTube forces you to watch some pre-roll ads before you can hit the Skip Ad button. Statistics are hard to come by, but it's logical to assume the time spent viewing a sponsored post on Instagram or Twitter is even less.

The smart companies know this and they work within the constraints to get the most bang for their advertising buck. If you've watched YouTube, you can easily tell which companies understand the game and how it's played. The best example, currently, are the Ok Google ads, made by Google themselves. Since Google owns YouTube, they made up the game and so they understand the rules on an intimate level. It's a skip-able ad, but you have to watch at least five seconds of it and the words "Ok Google" are used right about the four second mark. You *will* hear 'Ok Google" before you skip that ad.

Then there are the companies that don't get it at all and I'm looking at *you,* Motion Picture Association of America. Every movie trailer starts with a five second shot of a green screen with the rating information for the trailer itself. Then there's a black screen for approximately one second which serves to frame the trailer away from the green screen. After that, you'll likely see a card for the studio or studios involved and that takes one to two seconds. And finally, after all of that, the trailer starts… approximately eight seconds later.

Most people hit the Skip Ad button three seconds ago. They didn't watch the ad, they don't know which movie it's for, and *they don't care*. These ads completely fail online and it's no wonder. The movie industry creates trailers formatted to play in a cinema to a captive audience awaiting the start of a movie. YouTube viewers aren't captive, you want to make your ad money work, better get your point across in five seconds or less.

Given who and what I am, in this case a cyberpunk enthusiast with a penchant for the philosophy and history of the genre, I'm taken back to a far simpler time. A time when people weren't quite so jaded. The world was larger, and more mysterious. Technology was fascinating and a little scary. New things popped up everywhere! There were new ways to get music. There were new ways to watch television. There were new advances in video gaming. It was an exciting time fraught with fears and yet glimmering with hope.

You know, the 1980s.

A new character emerged onto the cyberpunk scene first as a movie star, then as a veejay, and then as a television star. He was one of the first publicly famous artificial intelligence concepts and his name was Max Headroom. For a computer generated AI, there was absolutely nothing computer generated about the character who first appeared in a 1985 movie called *Max Headroom: Twenty Minutes Into the Future.* Matt Frewer, the actor behind Headroom, spent more than four hours in a makeup chair to achieve a computer generated look. Since Max is an AI, he always appeared on a screen and sometimes multiple screens. Could be computer monitors or televisions or whatever. Behind him, there were swirling and moving geometric backgrounds which looked computer generated, but were actually painted by hand.

While Disney's *Tron* preceded Max Headroom by three years, *Max Headroom: Twenty Minutes Into the Future* was a television movie and they didn't have the budget for the same level of digital special effects.

One of the movie's plot points revolves around blipverts, a new form of television commercial designed to prevent people from channel flipping during station breaks. They were highly compressed ads, delivered at high speed, containing dense subliminal messages to buy the product. Blipvert side effects include confusion, headache, nausea, and the occasional explosion.

No really, watch the movie. That's what happens. Sometimes people explode when they see a blipvert. Oddly enough, blipverts last about 20 seconds. That's only ten seconds less than many television ads. Either way, blipverts are created to solve a problem, which is to keep people watching the ad in spite of the fact that they could flip to another channel while waiting for the ad to finish.

Today's problem is the same but the medium changed. You can watch videos on YouTube, Vine, Periscope, Vimeo, and Instagram and each one has their own set of users with their own channels. You can read up on what your friends are doing on Twitter, Facebook, Tumblr, and more and, once again, there are thousands of avenues on each. So the need to get that ad in front of you is real, and the need to compress it to the essential message is vital. Six second ads on Vine? Five second pre-rolls on YouTube?

That's just the start. Advertising is one of the most malleable mediums in the universe and if Madison Avenue needed to compress everything in to one second, they'd do it. It'll flash on your screen as you pass it. Buy this car. You need these shoes. See this movie. It'll be there and gone in an instant, a mere blip on your screen.

* * *

It doesn’t spoil the movie to tell you that Max Headroom and his colleagues win the day. Evil is defeated, good triumphs, and the blipverts end. The evil advertising campaign is over. Out here in the real world of 2015, the blipverts are just beginning.

There's a final, ironic twist to the tale of Max Headroom. The character was born in a movie about the twisted world of large corporations and the pursuit of money through advertising. So while Max was undoubtedly an iconic character of the 80s, he became one of the most ironic as the face of Coca Cola in the New Coke ads that made him famous worldwide.

By Using Your Site I Agree to Nothing

There's a disturbing trend I'm seeing among websites today, but before I get into that, let me describe the situation as if it happened in real life.

You're walking down the street past some shops, perhaps an outdoor mall like we have around Phoenix. You're not really looking for anything in particular, just browsing the shops and looking through their windows. You happen upon one shop with an interesting widget in the window and, pausing, you examine it more closely.

Suddenly, someone bursts from the shop and grabs you. They reach in your pocket and pull out your ID card. They make a quick note of it, verify your address to be correct, and explain that — because you stopped to look through the window — you've agreed to be tracked while in front of the store and possibly beyond if they find you an interesting sort who could be a potential customer. They force you to take a coupon that you don't want, and then they go back inside where they watch you closely through the window as you wonder what in the hell just happened.

That's what's going on with far too many websites today. I'm sure you've seen it too, a little box that pops up somewhere on the site that says something like "By using this website you agree to our use of cookies and their placement upon your computer in accordance with our cookie policy. You agree to be bound by the terms of our visitor agreement..." and so on. Some of these things contain perfectly legitimate information and have some legal basis in that they are telling you what their cookies are going to do and even how you can disable them. Yet there are plenty of them who posture that you're breaking their terms of service if you block cookies, or worse, employ an ad-blocker.

There's an old saying "the right to swing your fist ends at my nose." Moving that into the digital age, a website's right to present bits and information ends at my computer. My computer, and yours, is not an extension of any website. Once the bits land on your system, you have the right to say no to anything. How you do that is up to you and the mechanisms you employ. For me, my browser of choice is Firefox. So I use uBlock Origin along with Privacy Badger from the EFF to lock out all of the things I don't care to handle. There are other solutions out there and you can get very involved with controlling how websites interact with your computer.

Besides, there's one way around all of this that none of those "visitor agreements" seem to address: private browser or incognito mode. All modern browsers support some kind of privacy mode where nothing is saved or retained, not even the browsing history. I know more than a few people who browse like this as a default. So the private browser visits the site, supposedly agrees to their uses of cookies, and then the user closes out and nothing is retained.

Going one step beyond, what happens if I choose to block cookies? Can they sue me? Can they stop delivering content, services, and products to me? Will the site no longer come up if their software detects a cookie blocking agent? The answers, in order, are no, no, and no. Of course there's no legal basis for this behaviour because, first, they'd have to be able to prove someone was behind the keyboard. I could fire up a quick script that goes to a given website at a random point during the day on a computer I don't use. No one is at the keyboard, so no one can agree to the policy. The other two methods are easily defeated via private browsing. When you're incognito, every time you visit the site is the first time you've visited the site.

And you know what? I still use those websites. I'm not bound by their terms of service and neither are you. They have painted their screed on the wall of the Web and it's there for everyone to see and access. How you access it isn't for them to say because they accepted the terms of use of the Web when they put it online in the first place. You can post your message high and proud but, once it's out there, that message isn't yours anymore.

Life Lessons from the 8 Bit

My nine year old son has gotten into something rather surprising — 8 bit games for Nintendo and Sega. You know, the old stuff I used to play on the Nintendo Entertainment System or the Sega Master System. As I type this, he's in the office, playing *Contra* on a NES emulator for the Mac.

He's also doing the best he can not to swear and curse whenever he dies. In some ways, it's funny while it's also heartening to watch him not give up, but rather grit his teeth and wade back into the fray, spread gun blazing away at the turrets. As I watch him, and listen to him, I've also schooled him. He was having issues with one level, getting frustrated, and really working himself up into a good state of pissed-off. I told him to calm down, grabbed the controller out of his hand, and did a speed run through the level, killing *almost* everything that moved.

Thing is, I didn't kill everything. Oh no.

* * *

That's what I've been teaching him, that even video games can be a life lesson. Today's games are very different from the ones I played growing up. You see the latest game in the *Legend of Zelda* series? Holy crap it's pretty. Link, the main character, looks like an elven warrior. He's got his sword and shield at the ready. He's dynamic, ready for battle, and capable of bringing down the forces of Ganon yet again. He's got great moves that execute fluidly with a push of a button or a wave of the Wii-mote.

That's cool. The Link I grew up with looked like a small block of green squares… because he was a small block of mostly green squares

You can kind of see that he's an elf. His ear does look sorta pointy in the way that a square can look pointy. His nose? Yes, it's touching his shield and look at the size of it! (His nose, not his shield.) His foot barely extends from his leg and he's bereft of kneecaps. Now, does he have green eyes and huge brown eyelashes or does he have brown eyes with huge green eyebrows? Who knows? And who cares? This little green dude and I took down Ganon together.

It's not just the graphics though, is it? Games today barely even come with a manual and you know why? Because you're led through the game by the hand, pulled along by dialogue and invisible rails. Hell, I can name several games where one of the characters literally has the word "FOLLOW" over his head in big letters so you know to follow that bastard. Don't go off and do your own thing. Don't explore too far, because you need to follow that fool otherwise the game won't go anywhere. Almost any game you buy and play today will spend the first 15 minutes to an hour doing little more than teaching you how to play the game. Meanwhile, back in *Zelda,* you're dropped in a tan land surrounded by green rock

Where do you go? What do you do? Left? Right? Up? Is that a cave? Should you go in it? Where are you? You need to answer these questions yourself. In the original *Zelda,* there are dungeons, and it's best to explore them in a certain order as higher level dungeons require more life energy and better weapons. Trying to enter the level five dungeon right away after starting the game is suicide. Ah, but there's a snag:

Where in the hell is the level one dungeon, let alone level five? Where are *any* of the dungeons, and when you come to one, how do you know which level it is?

Short answer: You don't. Longer answer: You seriously need a map. Longest answer: You need a map, some intel on the land of Hyrule, and unless you have the little manual that came with the game, you don't get it. You. Are. On. Your. Own.

I love the game *Batman: Arkham City*. Flying around a big cityscape as the Dark Knight Detective? Solving crimes and kicking ass? Beating the shit out of Penguin and flirting with Catwoman? Hell yes, that's fun! Funny thing though. When you finally suit up as Batman, you get the following items:

* * *

- A map
- A wide selection of gadgets
- A wealth of abilities to kick ass
- Ranged weapons
- Smoke bombs
- Grappling hook
- Support from Alfred and Oracle

Meanwhile back in 8 bit land, Batman is dropped on a dark Gotham city street.

You don't get shit, Jack. You can beat up bad guys, you'll eventually get some Batarangs and gadgets, but when you start out you are naked in a Batsuit. Help isn't coming. No one will talk you through the level. You need to do this yourself.

So, going back to him playing *Contra,* what did he learn in a few minutes with a Nintendo game and his old man?

Sometimes, you are on your own. You make the decisions and you call the shots. Backup isn't coming. Because of that, you are liberated to do what you need to do.

I took the controller from him and did a speed run through that level. From that he learned that with experience and practice, you can do awesome and interesting things.

He also learned that you don't have to kill everything that moves. In real life, this equates to dealing with distractions. NES games were all about distraction. Don't let distractions keep you from accomplishing your goals.

Speaking of distractions, that guy down there? He can't shoot you from here. You need to go down there to shoot him, and when you go down there, you'll get shot. So if he can't bother you, why bother him? In the words of *Bad Street Brawler*, another old-school video game, "Never trouble trouble till trouble troubles you." He's just another distraction. Move on.

That turret that juts out of the rock? It can only shoot in 8 directions. If you're standing in a place that isn't one of those directions, then it can't hurt you. That weird gun that just appears out of the ground and fires off a burst of three rounds? You can lie down right in front of it and pump lead into it and it has no defense mechanism for that. The end boss of level one? Stand back with the spreader and fire away. It can't reach you on the far side of the screen and you can just poke away until you win. The lesson? Every problem you have to deal with has an optimal way of dealing with it. Find that optimal way and use it to your advantage.

The bridge that explodes out from under you? You'll land in the water below it and you're actually out of reach of many of the enemies that were pursuing you on the bridge. Sometimes the things that look like problems are just opportunities.

Throughout most of *Contra,* and many other games on the NES, there is no good reason to stop moving. Keep moving forward, and never take your finger off the trigger. While that might not be a perfect analogy for life, an easy metaphor is to keep moving forward and try to prepare for the things in your way.

For now, it's getting late. So the thing that he'll learn here in a few minutes is that the video game will be there tomorrow, and he can always conquer it then with a clearer head, made possible by a good night's sleep.

And always remember, if in doubt. UP UP DOWN DOWN LEFT RIGHT LEFT RIGHT B A START.

My Rocky Road to Linux

I've not always been a Linux user. In truth, it's something that I've fiddled with on and off for years, usually bouncing back to Windows when I was done with it or hit the limits of my knowledge.

Now, I use it on a mostly full time basis. My laptop is a dual boot Kubuntu / Windows 7 machine. Most of the time, if I'm in Windows, it's because there are a couple of games my kids play that only work in Windows. When they're done with it, I reboot into Kubuntu Linux and start working on the things I want to work on.

So what changed? What made me stay?

Well, that's the biggest part of my road to Linux. I've always loved the idea of Linux. Open source software as a philosophy suits my own personal philosophies of computer usage, but it goes deeper than that. As a librarian and technologist, open source software is a very attractive option for libraries. People aren't locked into Microsoft and libraries need not be locked into Microsoft licensing for the relatively simple needs of the typical library patron. Your average library user who needs a computer usually wants to do certain key things. They want to get online and check their email, social networks, and favourite websites. They want to write something on a word processor. They might want to listen to a song or watch the odd video on YouTube. Or they need to do all of these things — get online so they can research a paper that they'll have going in another window.

Nothing about those needs per-supposes a need for Microsoft anything. Don't get me wrong, as a slider, I love Windows and OS X, but libraries are notoriously cash strapped, so if they could save money on operating systems and volume licensing, all's the better.

Then again, you'll get the occasional patron who wants more. They want to do some photo editing. They want to put together a video. They want to design some kind of logo. They want to cut together and mixdown some audio. These things are certainly possible on a Windows workstation, but the software doesn't always work as well unless you buy the expensive stuff. So does one expect libraries to have workstations with Photoshop, Premiere, Illustrator, and Audition? None of those products are cheap.

Meanwhile, a technically minded library person could easily outfit a Linux workstation with all the necessities and do so for free. For writing and office related needs, there's LibreOffice. Want to surf the web? Chromium and Firefox are there for you. Need to do some multimedia work? No worries. For almost all of those patrons, GIMP, OpenShot or Kdenlive, Inkscape, and Audacity will work exceptionally well for them and will be more than they need for most of their projects.

But how did I end up using Linux full time? Well, like I said, the change was in the changes.

It was the late 90s when I first set foot into the Linux world. I had a friend help me set up Slackware. It was pretty cool, but not knowing a whole lot about Linux, I got stuck often. I hated bugging my friend all the time with what had to be simplistic, newbie questions. So I eventually went back to Windows because I had a far better understanding of it. A couple of years after that I tried Red Hat and then Mandrake. I liked both quite a lot but, if I recall correctly, Mandrake used an early version of KDE. Being a bit of an artist and designer, I loved the look. By this time, I was working at a public library and occasionally helping out in the IT department with some minor tasks. The head of IT was a good friend of mine. Heck, we played D&D on the weekends. While we used a Windows based ILS, he utilized thin client technology and Linux to deliver the ILS to staff on the public floor.

For those who don't know, an ILS is the integrated library system. It's the software that makes the library work, not only handling the checking in and out of materials but also the cataloguing and online aspects of the library's collection.

Being able to work with it in a practical setting greatly increased my overall knowledge of the operating system and, for a while, I ran Mandrake and KDE at home. However since this was the early 2000s, there were some simple things like software installation and dependency satisfaction that made things a little more difficult than they needed to be. Enthusiasts were already talking about "desktop Linux for everyone" but anyone who wasn't a fanboy could easily see that more work had to be done if regular people were going to see this as a viable alternative.

I gave up on it for a bit and concentrated on Windows. Buy that time I was in college and didn't have as much time to fiddle around with an operating system. I was busy working on a degree and figuring out a future. After college, however, I took another look at the open source landscape and by then there was this new thing called Ubuntu on the scene. My geek friends had a love/

hate opinion of it because they saw it as an easier road to Linux, but curiously didn't like it for the very same reason. I guess they figured that some of the exclusivity was going away if anyone could easily install and run a Linux distro.

So I gave it a shot and liked it. Being fresh out of college I didn't have a lot of money for a dedicated Linux system, so I ran it off and on as I could. Ubuntu was the first big change for me. It was the easiest distro I'd ever installed. There wasn't a whole lot of weirdness and, for all of my love for computers, there are times I just want things to work and work easily. So Ubuntu became my distro of choice. The great thing about it is that installing a separate desktop environment was as simple as knowing the apt-get command which was a welcome change, and that's the thing, the changes.

The changes were what made me switch on a permanent basis. While the ease of Ubuntu was a big change over the challenges of other distros, there was an online change in that Google appeared on the scene. When I first got into Linux, there wasn't a Google. There was a Yahoo, but it wasn't all that great. Now, let me lay out a scenario for you. Tomorrow I fire up my Linux laptop, log into KDE, and start working on something. I found out the day before there's a cool app I want to try. How did I find that out? Through one of the great online Linux websites now available online. I go to install it and, oh, it's not in the repositories for Kubuntu.

Meh, no problem. I'll Google up the PPA and add it.

That's the biggest change. I have a problem, I Google it. I don't have to rely on a couple of knowledgeable friends, I can rely on tens of thousands of knowledgeable friends. I can Google a solution because, since I'm not running anything weird and bizarre, there's no way my problem is unique. Hundreds of people have had my problem and hundreds helped solve it. As a librarian, it's almost poetic that I switched to Linux simply because the information is so ambiently available.

So here I am, I started this post on my Android tablet and I'm finishing it in Linux. At some point I'll have to replace this ageing laptop and I'm looking at something akin to an ultrabook, and chances are it'll be a Linux ultrabook. To be perfectly honest, if I could find a Linux laptop with a similar form factor to a 13 inch MacBook Air, I'd stop carrying my tablet all together.

But that's for later.

J Pop and the Non-Existent Language Barrier

As a student of Japanese Pop Culture, I often hear questions like "Dude, I love X about Japan, but why is Y so freakin' weird?"

I think a Japanese music video can, at least partially, answer that question. Let's pick one called PONPONPON by Kyary Pamyu Pamyu. It looks kind of strange, right?

But is this really so strange? I mean, okay, she's got a weird stage name. She's singing a somewhat bizarre, but happy tune. The music video features her dancing with toys, wearing strange makeup, while even stranger people dance in the background. So on YouTube and in other places here's that question:

"Dude, I love music videos, but why are Japanese music videos so freakin' weird?"

Simple, because she's singing in Japanese.

* * *

No seriously, that's it. That's the only thing that's absolutely foreign about this video. It's the only thing about this video that Westerners don't get. Because we fixate upon language, even if we don't speak it, and we tie that language to what's going on around it. Since language is such a huge part of our understanding of the world, if we don't get the language, we similarly do not get what's going on around it. Incidentally, that's not a Western trait, but a human trait.

She's speaking Japanese. That is the only difference between this video and American music videos. Nothing in the content of the video itself, visually, is different from anything you've ever seen in an American music video.

Don't believe me? Good. A little skepticism will take you far. Here's some proof.

Let's start with her name. Kyary Pamyu Pamyu. Sounds weird right? I mean, Pamyu Pamyu? What's up with that? My answer is I don't know, what's up with Lady Gaga? Lady Gaga is precisely the same kind of name as Kyary Pamyu Pamyu. It's a stage name, as Pamyu Pamyu's real name is Takemura Kiriko. That's actually a pretty common name. It's not quite the same as Jane Smith, but it's right up there. It's a common name, so she chose a stage name. One that's designed to set her apart from other people in her field doing the same kind of business. Would you buy music from Stefani Joanne Angelina Germanotta? I mean, who? Who the hell is Stefani Joanne Angelina Germanotta?

She's Lady Gaga.

She chose a stage name because her name doesn't exactly roll off the tongue. Like Pamyu Pamyu, her name is also a portrayal of a character. When Stefani (that's Gaga Stefani not Gwen Stefani) is in Lady Gaga mode, you expect something from her. You expect her to act like Lady Gaga. However, when Stefani is off-stage, maybe cruising around town and taking a day off, she's not Lady Gaga. If she's speeding and the police pull her over, the speeding ticket will not be made out to Lady Gaga.

In case you haven't figured this out by now, popular music is a lot like professional wrestling. These singers, these performers… they're performers. They are, in many ways, just like pro wrestlers. They portray a character in the media, on-stage, and in interviews. For many of them, indeed for most of them, that is not who they are in real life. Ke$ha? You know, the party hound who sings about brushing her teeth with Jack Daniels and getting laid on the dance floor?

She's a massive fan of Cold War history. She's snuck into college lectures to listen to professors talk about the history of the Cold War.

That's part of Kesha Sebert. It's not part of the persona that is Ke$ha.

Moving on, the makeup? The really weird makeup she wears in part of the video? Back to Lady Gaga, indeed back to Cyndi Lauper, back to Boy George, hell, let's go all the way back to

Josephine Baker. She's a performer. That's what she's wearing because she is there to get your attention and perform for you. The concept of striking makeup isn't at all weird in American or Japanese cultures and its manifestations in pop music isn't new either.

Maybe it's weird to some people that she's literally frolicking with toys. If that's the case, then I'm not sure why. Owl City does the same thing in the video for Fireflies. The White Stripes have a classic video done with nothing but stop-motion Lego. I think really good music videos invoke a sense of fantasy. That kind of thing seems appropriate when you're trying to bring music into a more physical, and visual, medium. Toys are child-like and they convey a sense of child-like wonder, or perhaps the innocence and fun of being a kid.

Perhaps it's the little dance she's doing. I can see how that might throw people. She's doing this bouncy-cutesy dance. Surely that's weird. Except it's not. In 1994 another bouncy-cutesy dance called the Macarena took over the world for about a month. More recently LMFAO proudly proclaimed that they're shufflin' not every-so-often, but every day. 2002 saw an international pop phenomenon from a girl group called Las Ketchup with a song titled Aserejé. What's a big part of the video? A bouncy-cutesy dance.

Let's keep digging, we're not quite there yet. What about the title? I've been asked about the titles of Japanese pop songs and why they're so different. Are they? I didn't really notice, actually. PONPONPON? So? What's so weird about that when the Black Eyed Peas had a big hit with Boom Boom Pow? Though people regret it now, a song by Crash Test Dummies burned up the airwaves in 1993. It's title: Mmm Mmm Mmm Mmm actually makes it hard to write about because I had to verify the number of Ms in each section of Ms. In 1980, the Police hit the top ten with De Do Do Do, De Da Da Da. Oh and that reminds me, remember Da Da Da by Trio? It's been used on several commercials and just won't seem to go away.

* * *

Finally, let's look at Kyary Pamyu Pamyu's attire, skipping over the fact that attire is just as much a part of a pop singer's act as is their music. Even in the realm of American pop, each star has their own look. Lady Gaga dresses nothing like Katy Perry who is distinct from Britney Spears who is now tame in comparison to Miley Cyrus who seems to be taking fashion cues from Rihanna. So we have little to talk about here after all. She's wearing an almost fairy schoolgirl outfit here, which is different from Britney Spear's sexy schoolgirl ensemble.

What I'm trying to say with all these examples is that 95% of the content here isn't different at all. It's presented in a novel way, certainly, but when you look at what's really going on, there's nothing in this video that hasn't been done in an American music video. Odd visuals and strange faces with juxtaposed non-sequitur while the singer performs the song? Peter Gabriel did it before her.

So the performer's name isn't all that

different. Neither is the title of her song. Her makeup isn't anything new or unseen in Western music videos, nor is her video's content. Even the fashion statement is almost subdued compared to a Rihanna or Madonna type of act. That leads us back to the only thing that's actually different about this video.

The language.

Every culture takes something and runs a different way with it. That's diversity. That's humanity. When it comes down to it, you could understand this video far better by learning Japanese. I'm not saying you need to, nor am I saying you should. I'm merely pointing out the thing separating Westerners from this video is a language barrier, not a content barrier.

Now Available in Mirrored

Of course they come in a mirrored style.

Say what you like about Google Glass, it's just another step into the future. It may be a misstep, it could be a stumble culminating in a fall, but that fall will happen with forward momentum. The idea of a device, whether worn or cybernetic, that projects information directly into your field of vision has been a staple of the science fiction and cyberpunk novel since *Neuromancer*. It's a trope, but there are reasons for that.

Information arrives and we are forced to look at a device. An audible tone or a soft vibration alerts us to new events and we fish around our pockets or belt clips to see what the deal is. Even with high definition screens, beautiful design, and sleek access; we're trapped holding a thing in a manner that allows us to gaze upon it. If only there were a better way.

There is, but it's not something we can quite

manage yet. It'd be perfect if that information were simply placed within our field of view. You have a new message. You're going somewhere? Here are a series of virtual arrows guiding you in the right direction. The time is 13:47 and it's 23 degrees C. Your parents' anniversary is tomorrow. It's all right there, in front of you. When it's right in front of you it's hard to ignore or forget. Don't want to miss an appointment? Make sure it's hovering in your eyesight with a countdown timer. That's the dream.

And it's coming true with Google Glass. Sure, people deride it while others praise the innovation it brings. For some it's stupid and for others it's amazing. He's a Glasshole, she's a Glasstronaut. It's all relative, but it's baby steps into what is undoubtedly the future. It's a future shaped by the past and by the science fiction that so often drives technological innovation.

In the realms of sci-fi, a creator's mind runs free. Limitations don't exist save for those the creator places upon their own speculation. If ever you feel sci-fi doesn't influence technology, take a look at the flip-phones of yesterday compared to *Star Trek* communicators in the 60s. Speaking of *Star Trek,* Uhura wore a single ear communicator that looks a hell of a lot like a Bluetooth earpiece. Touchscreens? Got those, but sci-fi was there first. From computer viruses to interplanetary probes, the science fiction writers talked about tech far in advance of it becoming reality.

Within cyberpunk, there are the mirrorshades. Indeed it was the title of a pivotal collection of short stories in the genre. I've worn them for years now, especially after landing in Phoenix, Arizona. Sunglasses are a basic necessity and they may as well be mirrored.

Today I read an article from The Verge about a fashion designer's take on Google Glass, and a smile crept across my face. Yet again, I saw the past in the future and another prediction made real. Of course there will be mirrorshade style Google Glass. It was foretold by science fiction that, all too often, becomes prophecy unto itself.

I never had a chance to see Homer and Jethro perform live and in concert.

It could have something to do with the fact that Henry Haynes, aka Homer, the rhythm guitarist half of the duo, died five yeas before I was born. Kenneth Burns, better known as Jethro, lived until 1989, but you really can't have Homer and Jethro without Homer. It was vinyl that gave me my first exposure to these two funny guys who played silly tunes decades before Weird Al Yankovic appeared on the scene. Grooves cut in plastic, read by a diamond needle that rustled along the peaks and valleys of the record. You can't get more analogue than the physical nature of what makes a record work.

But maybe I should back up a second and explain who and what I'm talking about. Homer and Jethro were two musicians who parodied popular country tunes from the 1940s on into the 60s when their popularity started to wane. In that time they entertained audiences on radio, television, and through records with their "educated hillbilly" nature which was borne of the fact that they were both *jazz* musicians, not country singers. Jethro played mandolin better than some of the greatest people in bluegrass and Homer has a style with rhythm guitar that I rarely see anymore. They're a classic duo and, since they were a part of my growing up, I feel a certain nostalgia for them.

Even though half of the group died years before I was born.

We live in an era unlike any other before. For the most part, you can call up a video-on-demand of most anything you want. You can listen to a song, any song, with just a couple of clicks. Want to watch the latest episode of Game of Thrones? You can do that. Want to watch the first episode of CSI: Miami? It's available somewhere. Want to read a book on your eReader, and fold that into the archive of hundreds of books on that eReader? No problem. You missed an episode of your favourite television programme? Actually you didn't. You remembered to set the DVR to record it a few days ago. You can watch it this weekend along with all the other shows you digitally recorded during the week.

But there was a time before this, and it wasn't all that long ago, that if you missed an episode of your show, *you* missed *it*. It was gone. Maybe you caught it in reruns later that year, but that was a matter of luck. You could go to the cinema and catch a movie, and maybe you enjoyed that movie. Maybe it became your favourite movie. You could go see it again, but when it left the cinema it too was gone. Unless they screened it later, it wasn't unusual to never see a given movie again. Videocassettes, DVDs, Blu-rays—they didn't exist.

What's worse is that so many things from this not-so-bygone era are gone. They've disappeared. They may have been destroyed, erased, overwritten, or just thrown away. The human race has a nasty habit of not taking care of our culture because, in many ways, we don't know that we're *making* culture when we're making it. The original episodes of Johnny Carson's Tonight Show, gone. The earliest episodes of Doctor Who — so many have been lost. London After Midnight, a horror movie starring the great Lon Chaney, disappeared. Hell, NASA and the United States lost the original recordings of the moon landings. Turns out they regularly erased the tapes for reuse later and no one thought that one of the greatest events in the history of civilization might be worth hanging on to.

A while back, some of the lost Doctor Who episodes surfaced in Nigeria. Some of the lost moon landing tapes were found, at least in copied form. The original tapes of Monty Python's Flying Circus were saved at the last minute when Terry Gilliam, a former member of the legendary comedy team, bought the master tapes just before the BBC wiped them. There's hope, and miracles occasionally happen.

What's worse is when something is lost, then found, but then we discover that the content is stored upon unreadable media. The technology needed to read the media has also been lost, or there's not a single working version of it anywhere in the world.

I had to wait until I was in my thirties before I ever saw one of my favourite musical comedy acts perform live. By that point, both of them were gone and with them my ability to ever see them perform. Thankfully, because someone thought to save some of those television performances, I was able to watch them, and it was amazing. See, any music fan will attest that you get so much more when you watch the musician do their thing. I knew that Henry played a mean rhythm guitar, but watching him, man.... There's more to it than playing rhythm guitar, it's how he did it so effortlessly.

Did you know that he chewed gum most of the time he was on stage? Henry would put it to the side of his mouth while singing but when Kenneth picked up a solo on the mandolin, Henry provided backing rhythm and chewed gum. Roddy Piper came to chew bubble gum and to kick ass, and he was all out of bubble gum. Henry came to chew bubble gum and to play guitar, and he brought extra gum just in case. I didn't know that, because you can't see that when you're listening to a record.

We achieved a kind of immortality when the human race learned how to write. Writing passes down thoughts, ideas, and knowledge through the eons and on to today. We have clay tablets from Mesopotamia that are over 5,000 years old. Yet we can read them and, because of that, we can summon a part of the author through the centuries and bring their thoughts with them. We did it again when we discovered how to record audio and video. Bela Legosi is dead, Bauhaus has assured me of this for years now. Yet I can see him right now if I want to. All I need to do is find him, and he's not hard to find. I can even find Lon Chaney, because someone recorded him.

But I can't find all of him. London After Midnight seems to be utterly lost to the mists of a semi-recent time — an artistic expression of our culture gone to apathy, misadventure, or plain old-fashioned stupidity. What survives today does so through a rather new process of achieving immortality.

Digital conversion.

When you have a digital file, you can manipulate it far more easily than you ever could anything else. Dubbing a vinyl record to tape takes time and special equipment. Converting an old record to CD is a pain in the ass. Converting a WMV (Windows Media Video) file into a more portable MP4 format? That takes seconds and requires little in the way of special equipment. Chances are if you have the equipment to *watch* the WMV file, namely a computer, you have all you need to convert it. Programmes like VLC will save it in another format. You can convert files in bulk. You can strip the audio off and make a separate file from that because you want to listen to it on your personal media device. All you need is software.

From there, we turn to a final method of immortality, which could actually be the first way we discovered to live forever—we share.

We live in a world where, as long as we can play the thing back or read the thing at all, we can digitize it and it never need disappear again. It can be copied out to thousands of sites. It can be backed up. It can be converted and ported to different things. Floppy discs went out of fashion so we put things on CD. CDs faded out, so we put things on flash drives. Now we can store it online in a cloud drive and make it accessible more widely than ever before.

So, long ago, many years before Henry Haynes died, someone pointed a camera and microphone at him and his partner Kenneth and pressed a red button. Performances were recorded on the media of the time, just like we do today. Today I shoot video on a camera with a solid state drive. Back then, it was magnetic tape. Those recordings of Homer and Jethro survived and someone with a computer finally got their hands on them, decades later. They fed the recording to the computer, converted analogue content into digital, and then they did what millions of people do everyday with digital video.

They uploaded it to YouTube.

All of the knowledge on the planet is worthless until it's shared. That's one of the many reasons I found myself working in a library, because knowledge is power and, while it may sound idealistic; power to the people, man. In the end, Homer and Jethro didn't live for years beyond their death because someone recorded a performance. I wasn't able to watch them because someone converted that recording into a digital format. I was able to finally, after over 30 years of fandom, watch them play live because someone shared that file. Homer and Jethro, Bela, Lon… they all died before the Internet, but we can experience them today through the various methods used by humanity to keep people alive even after they're gone. All of them are important, but not as important as that last one.

Remember someone or something today, someone or something that's gone. Then remember that it's not completely gone because you know about it. Then, finally, keep it alive.

Share it.

We live in an age where I can take a note on my iPhone and, in seconds, that note will appear on my Android tablet, my Linux laptop, my Windows server, my Windows laptop at work, and my Mac Mini. Not only can I capture a thought, I can replicate it many times over, providing a redundancy in both the back up and communication of my thought. Even if it's just a simple note to myself, I'll be able to pick up that note on any computer I own, or any place I can access the web.

More than that, I can easily share my thought with another. All I need to do is trigger the sharing feature within the note-taking app and suddenly my thought is also my friend's thought. I use Evernote, but there are plenty of others which do the same exact thing with a very similar feature set.

I use Evernote for quite a lot. Hell, I write stories, blog posts, essays, and articles in Evernote because it's a fairly secure place that, like I said before, works everywhere. I can sit in front of my Android tablet at Giant Coffee down the street in Downtown Phoenix, typing up a new blog post on the Bluetooth keyboard. I finish my coffee, leave, head for home, and then sit down at my computer and pick up exactly where I left off.

That's power. That's a lot of power over your ideas and your creativity.

Yet, sitting next to my keyboard right now are two things I don't care to live without: A spiral notebook and pen. Yes, dead trees and ink.

So you might be thinking, "What the hell? All that useful tech and you've got a spiral notebook?" Yes, and it's a fairly cheap one too. Say what you want about the really nice Moleskine notebooks, I've found that the lines in my spiral notebook are just as straight, just as horizontal, and I can write on them just as well for about $15 less than a Moleskine. I'm looking for a place to take notes, not an "experience."

* * *

But the question remains, why would someone who's so digitally inclined use something so antiquated as a spiral bound notebook? I've given that a lot of thought, because I don't claim to fully understand myself or my proclivities and I think it boils down to a few key things that, at least in my opinion, my notebook has over a digital device.

1. As much as I love Evernote, I have to launch it. No matter what machine or device I'm on, I have to invoke Evernote. My brain is such that I will have an idea that I really want to write down so I remember it, and in the space of time that Evernote takes to launch (one to two seconds) I can lose it. Yes, it can happen that fast. I'll think "Hey that's a good idea!" and if I don't write it down immediately, it could go from good idea to "I wonder what we're doing for dinner tonight?" My notebook is "always on." It's always there, it's launched, and literally on my desktop at all times. It's not an icon that launches my notebook, it is my notebook and it is ready to go now.

* * *

2. The randomness pleases me. Evernote is very organized, which pleases my librarian and scientist brain. My notebook isn't very organized, which is pleasing to my creative and artistic brain. Think of it like this, and perhaps you know someone very much like this. There's a guy, and he's an accountant. You go to his job and you'll find everything in place. His books are right there, his desk arranged just so. Computers and calculators are ready, pens and pencils in drawers, small pad of paper ready for jotting down a quick phone number. Then he goes home. His home is nicely arranged as well. It's been a long day, but he wants to work on that toy box for his niece. He's a woodworker, not a pro, but he knows how to build some lovely things. So he heads out to his wood shop — and it's an absolute mess. Stuff is everywhere. Tools laying all about, sawdust on the floor, wood stacked haphazardly on a workbench. Yet he's able to pick up his project and seems to instinctively know where that chisel is, or where the hammer is. He barely looks away from his project to pick up another tool because, even

though everything looks chaotic, it's chaotic because he's making something.

That's when you suddenly realize, it looks chaotic to you because you don't know how he works. The way I see Evernote is that it's a very structured place to write, keep articles, and organize my thoughts so that I can act on them. I see my notebook like that guy's woodshop. I know where stuff is and, even if I don't, I can find it pretty easily. It looks chaotic to you because you don't know how my notebook works. My notebook is where I can build things and Evernote is where I can put things into production.

3. Notes are not created equally. My Evernote tends to get the really important stuff. Things I want to read, things I need to act on, stuff I want to build, stuff I'm writing, and so on. My notebook tends to get everything. Important stuff will get transferred to Evernote so I can see it while I write or work, but for every note I add to Evernote, there are probably 20 more in my notebook that I'll jot down, look at, do or disregard, and then move

on. Looking at a page here I've got names of videos I want to check out, an architecture of a dropdown menu system on a site I'm working on, some planning notes for upcoming articles, a list of people who sent me email while I was on vacation, a blog post idea, the name of a singer I wanted to remember, and oh look, Daft Punk has a new song on Spotify.

That crap doesn't need to go into Evernote. Once I'm done with the videos, the dropdown menu setup, organising the articles, replying to the emails, writing the blog post, and checking out Yael Kraus (the singer I wanted to remember) on Spotify—I'll move on. I don't need a digital record of that stuff.

In the end, it comes down to what you need versus what you want. My notebook is full of wants, tonnes of them. I want to see that movie, I want to download that video, I want to remember that thing. My Evernote has that article I need to write, that website I need to check out because it's related to my job, that article I need to read because I’m certain I can learn something.

The paper notebook may be antiquated, but then again, so are wheels and I don’t see us giving them up any time soon for the same reason I’m not giving up my spiral notebook — it’s just too damn useful.

I was talking to a good friend last night about writing and why I write in so many places. I'll post the occasional essay here but I also write about libraries and technology on my professional blog. I also host a podcast over there and I write for that too, which is different than writing for a blog. I write books, and those books were borne out of two different websites as well.

I'm working on my third book now, which will be about cyberpunk, cyberculture, and the realisation of technology. Like the other books, I'm writing about this online and will eventually gather up these bits and pieces and shove them, kicking and screaming, into a single document which will become an eBook. This is nothing new in the world of tech and, as a matter of fact Paul Thurrott, one of my favourite tech writers, did this with one of his books.

Rather than collecting them under one banner, I'm publishing them on Medium, where there is a rather nice cyberpunk community.

Back to my friend for a minute, though, and why I write in so many places. The fact of the matter is that this blog isn't the place for everything I write, neither is Cyberpunk Librarian, or Medium. I also have a Tumblr site I will be updating more often as I work on my fourth, yes, fourth book. I wouldn't write about library stuff here and I wouldn't really write about deeper cyberpunk philosophy on my professional blog. Likewise, a lengthy essay and critique about Deep Throat doesn't really belong on Medium, and certainly not my professional site. It's all about niches, and the Internet is full of them.

My "problem," if you will, is that I like to write about a wide variety of things. Science, tech, porn, art, culture, books, libraries, and reflective personal things. If something interests me, it's a good bet I'll write about it sooner or later. I don't think it's unreasonable, or even unusual, to write specific things in specific areas. After all, the people going to my library site aren't the same people who will show up here. The people going to my library site are probably interested in libraries and tech and want to read stuff about that. They're not landing on that blog expecting to see an in-depth look at a classic porn film, nor should they see that there. There are plenty of other places to pick that up if the interest exists.

Back in the day, there was this phenomenon called "pulp magazines." These contained stories about all kinds of topics and genres but each magazine focused on a specific genre. They were called pulp magazines because they were printed on some of the cheapest paper possible to keep the price down. It wasn't unusual for a pulp writer to diversify their presence in the market. Writers like Robert E. Howard (*Conan the Barbarian*) and Lester Dent (*Doc Savage*) sold fantasy, western, historical, spicy, and adventure stories to the magazines that would buy them.

In many ways, I consider myself a pulp writer, the only difference being that I write essay and non-fiction. However, there's a parallel between my drivel and their writing — the way we speak to our audience. Like a pulp writer, I direct my words to everyone. I try to write so anyone with a degree of literacy in American English can pick up my stuff and get something out of it. Hopefully people enjoy it and hopefully they'll want to read more of my typing.

And hopefully, I've put it in the proper place for the reader to find it — filled the right niche, you might say.

Long ago and far away I walked away from MySpace. There were a number of reasons leading me to this decision. I mean, it was bad enough with the themes some applied to their accounts that induced seizures in people who don't even have epilepsy. Then there were all the pages that played music just as soon as you opened them. Nothing like a little late night browsing when suddenly, death metal erupts from your speakers. Then there was the fact that MySpace had an identity crisis in that it couldn't seem to figure out if it was a chat facility, a blog, a pre-Twitter Twitter-like service, or whatever the hell it was. Tom was friends with everyone and few people knew who he was. At the end of its run, MySpace was kind of ridiculous.

But in the end, I walked away for a very simple reason. I wasn't getting anything out of it and no longer felt it was something for me. I've done this with lots of things: books, TV shows, podcasts, musicians, and so on. I'm not condemning them or saying their work sucks, I'm walking away because I think it's no longer something I want. There were lots of people on MySpace when I left, and they didn't crumble for a long time.

So... Facebook

According to my profile page, I have just over 200 friends on Facebook. This includes real-life friends, online friends, family, people I kinda know, and people I've known forever. I love them all, I seriously do. But you know what?

Facebook just isn't anything I want anymore.

There are tonnes of reasons for this, just like there were with MySpace. First, there's the huge creep factor in the way Facebook mines my data to sell me things I don't need. The sad fact is that most, if not all, of these ads are absolutely useless to me. I just turned off Ad Block Plus, just as an experiment to see what Facebook thinks I'm into.

* * *

Keep in mind, I'm a nerd. I like space, and science, and computers, and books, and video games, and so on. Going down the ad list here I see:

> Tool specials at NAPA auto parts (I couldn't fix a car if you held a gun on me.)
> Superior Cleaning (Because apparently I need a pressure washer.)
> G-Star sale. (I literally have no idea what the fuck this is.)
> American Express (NO.)
> Braun electric razor (I've not used electric in over a decade, but I can explain this one… it's because I posted something about Dieter Rams a while ago. Who'd he work for, again?)

So yeah, nothing there and I mean literally, there's nothing there for me.

The content is okay, but over the last two years, the signal to noise ratio has increased to a shrill crackle and squeal over the occasional message in chaos. Anymore, It's not unusual to totally miss pictures of my grandniece or hear about someone's new job because of weird news stories and, oddly enough, pictures of how hot it is… in Phoenix.

As I write this, I'm looking out the window of my studio-office. Yup, can confirm, it's hot outside. A bit windy too.

This is not the fault of my friends or family. They are absolutely free to post the things they want to post and that's what they should do. Perhaps there are ways to apply a squelch to that noise and re-gain the signal all too often lost within the cacophony of "I took a quiz and I'm this Star Wars character" and "Everything Bad is Because of Liberals." (Or was it conservatives? Maybe my friends and family will wake up one day and realize that the government, as an entity, is broken. Blaming the left and/or the right for the breakage is like blaming your speedometer for your car's inability to start.)

* * *

Privacy and everything else

A while back, some fuckheads, and fuckheads they were, commented on a post I'd made. I had no idea who said fuckheads were. Never heard of them, didn't know them. Turns out, that post was public and open thanks to a new privacy setting that Facebook turned on and, apparently, I missed Facebook's notice of this new addition. Or it could be that I missed this notice because it never existed. I eventually learned about the issue from a tech news website where I also learned how to disable it.

Ladies and gentlemen, friends and family, Facebook is going to keep screwing with your privacy and continue making it harder to manage said privacy on Facebook. Like Kobe beef you are well fed, well pampered, coddled, massaged, to eventually be served on a plate with a parsley garnish to advertisers. Ads drive the web, I know this and accept it.

There's a difference between consent and

rohypnol in your drink.

Still, in the end, none of those reasons really add up to the one big reason I'm walking away from Facebook. It's the same thing and shouldn't be a surprise to anyone: It's not something I want anymore.

Does this mean I'm killing my Facebook account? Nuking it all from orbit and walking away in slow motion as it explodes behind me? No. I didn't do that for MySpace either. I simply stopped using it. It's like that TV show that went south last season and dammit, you know it went south. So you just, you know, stopped watching it. I've got some services set to post to Facebook for people who might have the interest, all ten of them I believe. Maybe twelve, it's hard to tell. I'll pop in to see family pics and check out what's going on in my neighbourhood because my neighbourhood has a Facebook page that's part news feed, part gossip magazine. And I'll keep Messenger on my phone for the people who use that to contact me. (My father doesn't really know, or care, how to text me. He knows how to hit me up via Messenger though.)

In short, I become a Facebook deadbeat. Facebook is there to sell ads and deliver them to me, targeting my proclivities based upon the information I post. In other words, what I post should become fodder for ads that people pay Facebook to show me.

But I won't see them.

It's a one-way communication line for the most part because my blogs, my feeds, the occasional news story — that will all still get posted here. But I won't see the results of it. Go ahead, like it. Comment on it. Facebook loves that. But the data and metrics generated from those posts and translated to ad delivery? I'll get none of it.

It doesn't really matter. I've never bought anything from a Facebook ad anyway. The advertising tended to be lost to apathy and Ad

Block Plus.

Follow me... everywhere but

So, if you care and if you want to follow me online, well — I know this may be hard to believe for some people — but there is a Web and an Internet outside of Facebook. I'm still active on blogs and social networks. I'm just not going to be hanging around Facebook much anymore. If you want to see what I'm up to, you can actually just stay here. All the stuff I posted that went to Facebook will still come to Facebook. That includes Twitter, Instagram, blogs, and so on. However, if you're daring, you'll follow me and others elsewhere.

- Twitter
- Google+
- Cyberpunk Librarian
- My podcast
- YouTube (New vlogs coming soon!)
- Instagram
- Hangouts

- Medium

Look at that! There's a vast online world out there beyond Facebook! Let's go exploring.

If the sky above the port was the colour of television tuned to a dead channel, then the sky above the Internet is cloudy.

With all the talk of clouds, cloud services, cloud storage, cloud solutions, cloud servers, and so on; you'd almost forget that the term isn't actually anything new. Those of us who are old enough, and geeky enough, to remember flowcharting can look back on our experience and remember that a cloud was often used to depict the Internet. The square icon would connect to a diamond icon which branched off to a cylindrical icon and a cloud icon. The cloud was the online world, where things could be stored and it didn't matter how.

So referencing the Net as a cloud isn't as new as some might think. That's been around ever since people planned programmes with lines and pictures.

* * *

Today we're encouraged, incentivized even, to store our data in the cloud. Our apps use the cloud, draw from the cloud, and push to the cloud. The first draft of this article? I wrote it on an iPad using the Google Docs app which saves the document, as I type it, to the cloud. Google's cloud service drives much of my online life, actually. For better or worse, I've accepted Google as The Lord and Savior of my drafts, photos, social networking, news, email, and so much more. I use Google Drive on damn near everything from my desktop at work to my MacBook Air to my Galaxy Note 3. Google Now knows me better than I do myself.

But it doesn't have everything, and it never will.

Cloud storage is incredibly cheap right now. I can get a full terabyte of storage on Google Drive for ten US dollars per month. Ten dollars a month for a terabtye? Sounds, great, right?

Or is it?

* * *

See, I have this philosophy that I will only give up control to so much data. My online life and my existence within the physical realm are closely intertwined. So when it comes to data and the hoarding thereof, I've found a far better pricing plan for storage. It's a fantastic deal. I get one terabyte of storage: I can add more storage at any time for a nominal fee: I can store anything from music to movies, documents to eBooks; and I have access to it anytime I need it. The transfer rate is insanely fast. At the time I subscribed to it, there was an initial payment of $110, but prices have dropped since then. It's even cheaper to get into the same plan at the same level of storage. Best of all, it's all under my control with strict access to who can access it.

Oh and there's no monthly fee and no transfer limit because what I "subscribed" to was a one terabyte, USB 3.0 external hard drive.

I want you to look at your digital life and ask yourself a very basic, but profound question. "Do I really need to put all of this stuff online?" Where do you access your data, and I mean the data you really want? Your digital movies, books, music, photos and so on? Do you think it's a good idea to put a ripped DVD on Google Drive or Dropbox? Of course not, even if it's pulled from your media you know that putting ripped (or pirated) stuff on a cloud drive is probably not the smartest move. You're going to keep that on a hard drive, or a USB stick, or something that's off line.

So if you're going to do that for some data, why not most of it?

My cloud drives are conduits. They act as transfer mechanisms for moving data from one system to another. While I do keep keep a very small amount of data on Google Drive, it's stuff I'm going to blog about very soon. In other words, all of it is going to end up on the front page of a website sooner or later. It's not like it's super-private. The primary reason my Google Drive exists is because I use a MacBook to do my job. That may sound weird, but when you realize that

I'm using a Mac in a library where everything runs on Windows, it makes more sense. I can create a graphic in Pixelmator (my image editor of choice) and then pick up the JPG on the web server running Windows Server and IIS. Right tool, right job.

The drive goes into my bag when I'm done and that bag is always with me when I'm using my computer. If you have your data readily accessible, when you want it, as you want it… then there's little difference between a cloud drive and a hard drive. It all comes down to monthly payment plans, of which the hard drive hasn't any.

As the corporations get bigger, their control grows. There's no good reason to give them everything and, when you get down to it, there's no good reason to give them anything. It's always up to you.

If there's anything that Americans love more than baseball and firearms, it's a sex scandal. Robin Williams said that America was founded by Puritans, people so uptight that the British kicked them out. For a country that's supposed to be a world leader in progressive thought and a global tastemaker, the United States' attitudes about sex remain firmly rooted in 17th century Puritanical Christianity. If the reader will forgive another quote, then I offer something from award winning actress, singer, and boxer Marlene Dietrich: "In America sex is an obsession, in other parts of the world it is a fact."

Americans can take a special kind of schadenfreudian glee in an age of inexpensive tech married to the Internet with the both participating in a wild threesome with social networks. Simply stated, it's easier than ever before to have yourself a really good sex scandal.

Think of the changes we've seen in just a few

years. It wasn't long ago that VHS was the norm and if you wanted to pirate a movie, you needed two VCRs, not a computer. The technology whipped around in a strange 180 degree turn where we went from magnetic tape rolling past a stationary, spinning reader to a stationary, spinning disc perched above a moving laser. Now, that's not such a thing anymore since movies are more or less downloaded or streamed over the Net. There are those who love DVD and Blu-Ray, but there are millions more relying on Netflix and less legitimate sources of entertainment.

Before now, if you liked a movie on VHS you either pirated a copy for a friend or allowed them to borrow the tape. If your Jolly Roger was flying high and you went down the road to piracy, their copy of the tape wasn't as good as the original. Analogue to analogue coping is usually lossy, and copy degradation noticeably set in after the second generation of freebooting.

That's not a problem anymore. Downloaded a movie and want to share with a friend? They can have a copy that's 100% true to the original, bit by bit, pixel for pixel. Not only that, they can have it quickly. Put it in a cloud drive, share it on a portable hard disc, or torrent it. It's free and easy and a video can travel worldwide in hours or minutes if it goes viral.

The American appetite for sex and scandal came to a head in 1995 with one of the first, and biggest, viral sex videos ever. In 1995 there was no YouTube or it's pornographic equivalents. Social networks hadn't been invented. The computer BBS was still viable and instead of getting online with a world wide web, people were calling other people's computers directly to leave messages and play text based adventure games. Cell phones weren't smart and they looked like a brick with the weight to match. Access to high speed computer networks were limited to workspaces and universities. The Internet hadn't become popular, but it was there, slowly growing in the background.

And between nerds on a Linux/Unix

powered Net and normals on CompuServe and AOL, a video — or clips therefrom — circulated among lecherous stares and chortling disapproval. The content was completely pornographic, yet it simply depicted a newlywed couple making love and having a good time. Nothing would have come of it if not for the stars. The woman was well known for her role on a popular television show at the time and her husband was the drummer for a hit-making heavy metal band. While the sex and drugs are well known contributors to rock and roll, the news media was shocked, shocked I tell you, at the Pamela Anderson and Tommy Lee sextape.

Were they?

Of course not. It was a media feeding frenzy of the highest order. Here was a woman who played a sex bomb on *Baywatch* where she typically ran around in a skin-tight one piece swimsuit and the drummer of Motley Crue. They're married, newlywed, on a lavish vacation, and fucking like most people do. There wasn't anything kinky, indeed the man kept telling her how much he loved her. If they hadn't been celebrities, I think the population at large would've considered it a boring porno. God knows there was far better porn out there as the 90s saw a renaissance in adult film making as porn began to go truly mainstream.

But the juicy details: Her legs splayed open while he pumped his throbbing member in and out of her neatly shaved pussy. (While they both professed their love for each other.) The media was quick to jump on the idea that this sex kitten was, oh my god, *actually a sex kitten.* (On a romantic and sensual honeymoon.) They were doing filthy, nasty things to each other. (For instance, she actually gave her husband a blow job.) America was all over it. Hot, sexy celebrities having hot, sexy sex!

It was a Pandora's box. The video went from server to server, user to user, and from inbox to inbox. It became a viral hit in another way as hackers wrote malicious programmes to take advantage of people wanting to see the video. CLICK HERE TO WATCH PAM FUCK TOMMY! proclaimed the link in the email, and suddenly you had a virus. The taste was on the tongue and the American public wanted more.

Now, thanks to Pamela and Tommy's tape, the release of a sex tape isn't so much of a scandal as it is a marketing decision. Actor Rob Lowe, billionaire heiress Paris Hilton, disgraced skater Tonya Harding, disgraceful musician Fred Durst. There are so many celebrity sex tapes and some of them weren't stolen so much as shot with the intention to sell on the open market. Professional wrestler Chyna made a porno with X-Pac, her pro wrestler lover at the time. Teen mom star Farrah Abraham made a sex tape that was purported be stolen, but then everyone noticed that her "boyfriend" was porn star James Deen.

Ask Kim Kardashian, who's famous because she's famous. If your ratings are down in the dumps, go down on your boyfriend or husband and make sure someone is filming it.

Then, my friends, everything got easier in the late 2000's. Cell phones became smart phones and they had cameras on them. Some of them have good cameras on them, too. Then along came the cloud storage solutions like Dropbox, Apple's iCloud, or Microsoft's OneDrive. (OneDrive was once SkyDrive which used to be Microsoft Mesh and, well… names can be so messy in a global economy.) Today, when I set up a new phone or tablet, I'll install one or more of these services on it. I use all of them in some form or another and, funny thing, no matter what I install them on all of them all of them ask the same question.

"Would you like to automatically send all of your photos to our cloud storage service?

Dropbox, OneDrive, Google Drive, and iCloud all offer options to take all the photos on your phone, and all of the photos that you take with your phone, and send them cloud-ward for backup and storage. It's a great idea. You can rest assured that those photos you took on your vacation are safe. Those photos you took when you visited your cousin in Hawai'i? They're are safely backed up on a cloud drive somewhere. Those photos of your kids playing on the beach? Don't worry, they're safe on a remote server. Those pictures you took standing just below Mauna Kea? You can edit them when you get home and just pull them down from the cloud.

Oh, and those photos you took of yourself standing naked in front of a mirror so you could show off your tanlines on your beach bunny body? Don't worry. Those are up in the cloud too.

In the 80s, people used Polaroids for porn. Hustler magazine had a section called Beaver Hunt where they encouraged people to send in pictures of their girlfriends and wives naked. Almost all of these pictures were Polaroids because, after all, you didn't need to take a Polaroid picture to a chemist for development. You didn't have to shoot a whole roll of film. Two or three snaps, pick the best one, send it to Hustler.

Or don't, maybe you just wanted a picture of your lover. It was easy, inexpensive, and no one would see it but you.

Digital cameras destroyed Polaroid instant photos and then smartphones came along and upended the digital camera market. The average iPhone has a camera on it that, while it isn't the best digital camera on the market, it's certainly good enough for millions of people. The pictures you take with your smartphone are easy and inexpensive.

And now, if you're not careful, absolutely everybody can see them.

iPhones will happily share your pictures to iCloud. Android will gleefully share your pictures to Google Photos. Use the Flickr app? Your photos can be automatically uploaded. Use Dropbox? OneDrive? All of these apps practically beg you to share your photos and store them on their services. Many of them will actually give you bonus storage space just to encourage such activity.

Before now, someone wanting to steal a picture of someone naked had only one vector: Break into their house, find the pictures, and steal them. Now, a resourceful hacker can get them from a cloud service, as most of the pictures associated with The Fappening came to be stolen from iCloud.

For those unfamiliar with the term, The Fappening was an event where not one, not two, but multiple and many celebrity pictures were stolen by hackers and posted online. While it's reasonable to believe that the hackers stole and posted entire collections of vacation snaps, selfies, and pictures of lunches; the real gold were the pictures celebrities took of themselves in the nude or, in a few cases, while having sex. The term, based upon the title of M. Night Shyalaman's lousy sci-fi movie, *The Happening*, The Fappening exposed more than several celebrities' genetalia. It exposed the flaws in a system where we can share anything and everything digital in a manner so easy, we cease to understand it.

It sounds weird to think that something is so easy that one wouldn't understand it, but think about it. When you drive your car, you turn your steering wheel, and your car moves in that direction.

How does that work?

No really how does that work? Do you really understand the electronic interlinks inherent in power steering and computer controlled traction assistance? You're no longer simply turning a series of shafts and gears that turns some more shafts and gears that move your front wheels in a particular direction. That's stuff your grandparents did. Modern cars are computer assisted and, in some cases, computer controlled. Turning your steering wheel suddenly involves binary and logic. Do you understand that?

Probably not. You turn the wheel, the car moves in that direction. You take the picture, you can pick it up on Dropbox later.

And so can anyone else that gains access to your Dropbox, iCloud, or whatever else. The vectors for attack have increased several fold. Your nudie pics no longer live in a drawer, or a photo album on a high shelf. They're effectively in someone else's photo album on someone else's high shelf in someone else's apartment. But it's okay, they promised to take good care of them for you and no one else will see them. Hand on heart.

Our smartphones are our lives and they carry images of our bodies if we allow them to. Think about it; with a modern smartphone, you hold your credit card, passwords, email, contact list, personal information, pictures of loved ones, combinations to your safe at home and at work, logins for Amazon and that little store that you don't tell anyone that you shop at. Your phone can be your life, and if you lose it, it's a nightmare to lock it all down and get it all back. That's why so many smartphones now offer some kind of, for lack of a better term, self-destruct feature.

Lose the phone and you can log into an account from a computer and turn it into a paperweight, wiping all the data and making it unusable to the thief. It's the nuclear option, but better to kill it from orbit than to let a stranger have access to your personal data.

That's the thing, smartphones aren't inexpensive and the better they are, the more money it'll take to replace them. Yet most of us prefer to turn it into an unusable piece of technology rather than risk someone taking what's on it. The celebrities who found themselves violated and exposed through the Fappening, however, didn't get this option. The phones were merely the path to vulnerability, capturing and uploading their images to iCloud and other online storage services.

Before two factor authentication became more common, all a hacker really needed was a username and password and they were in. Through phishing or brute force attacks, they got in, and they got everything they wanted. Rumours abound that there are more images and videos that weren't released on August 31, 2014, and I believe that.

The mobile age offers us a new frontier in personal computing. Your files were safe on your computer at home because it was at home. It might be hooked to the Net, but the connection was mostly outgoing and few people ran anything like a server in their home. Today, Dropbox, iCloud, OneDrive, and the others – these are all file servers. They're easy to use, and they lack the features of the enterprise versions of file servers, but they're file servers all the same. When a hacker doesn't need to access your computer or your phone at all to get things you don't want someone else to have, you're faced with a new question for a new century.

Is this information so important that I should put it on my devices, or is it so important that I shouldn't?

World Order

If there is any one reason I love the Internet it's because of the discovery. The fact is, I've discovered so much simply because someone shared it. World Order is no different. It started with an animated gif of Japanese guys in business suits dancing robotically, but in a way I hadn't really seen before. Robot dancing styles are nothing new but the fact that there were more than a couple, indeed there were seven, dancers was something different. They had their presentation tight and their moves were amazing.

And they're Japanese guys in business suits.

The gif was presented without context, as a funny thing on Reddit. Thankfully, because it was on Reddit, there was someone there to provide the context which I desired so badly. The commenter pointed out that this was a sort of Japanese techno group called World Order and the dance was from a music video for a song called Machine Civilization. You could check it out on YouTube.

* * *

Naturally, I did. Then I spent the next hour or so watching and listening to anything World Order that I could find and, because it's the Internet, I could find a lot of it.

As things go, Machine Civilization is a perfect introduction to World Order because it sets you up for much of the group's underlying themes. There's a positive message throughout their work and a recurring idea of "We are all one" that's pervasive in their music and videos. You get a feel for the flavour of the group and how they're serious about what they're doing, without taking themselves too seriously. It was enough to prompt some research into the whole thing and see what this was about.

The first fact stunned me, and then everything seemed to fall into place from there.

I've never claimed to be normal and, while I dislike violence, I enjoy professional fighting. I love boxing, martial arts, Muay Thai, and mixed martial arts. I don't jump up and down while shouting "HIT HIM! DRIVE HIM INTO THE FLOOR!" but a beer and a fight is a good time in my world. So it surprised me that I didn't recognize the lead singer of World Order. He didn't look familiar, but then I'm not used to seeing Sudo Genki wearing glasses and the garb of a sarariman.

Sudo is a retired mixed martial arts champion and I've seen him fight many times. During his MMA career, he was known for lavish entrances with music and lights and choreography — something you'd see in professional wrestling rather than serious MMA. From wearing a KFC helmet that blew its stack to dance moves he'd later utilize as front man for World Order, everyone knew when Sudo Genki was approaching the ring. Likewise his unorthodox approach to fighting, like actually having fun while doing it, led to many opponents underestimating him. They thought he was a clown, an idiot.

* * *

They usually changed their minds after waking up on the mat or just about the time Sudo locked in a submission hold.

Another piece that fell into place was the "We are all one" philosophy laced into the workings of World Order. More than once, Sudo displayed a banner bearing the same words in the ring after a victory. Maybe this all sounds strange, or even a little too television mystic for you. Is he reflecting a Kwai Chang Caine character or is he for real? Is this another game?

No. He's a practicing Buddhist, he's absolutely serious.

So in 2009 we have a Japanese fighter and Buddhist who retires from the ring and creates a music project. Why not?

Along with six other guys, Sudo continued the spirit of showmanship he displayed in the ring. It was something new—an ex-fighter who sings techno and dances with slick robotic choreography and sings about, oh my god; peace, harmony, and happiness.

The entire thing struck me as a weird amalgam of something straight out of a cyberpunk book, though the reasons may make sense only within my mind. Nevertheless, I think there's a social commentary in World Order that lends itself well to cyberpunk related entertainment.

The concept of a street samurai was there from the beginning. Molly Millions in Gibson's Sprawl Trilogy is the prototype from which all cyberpunk street warriors were built. She's everything we expect in a street samurai—intelligent, cunning, adaptive, suspicious, and occasionally ruthless.

Interesting, because those are some highly desirable traits of a businessperson too.

Sudo is a fighter who is taking on the worlds of business and government on his terms, all the while dressed in their garb. In another video,

Permanent Revolution, World Order brokers peace between Asian powers. Japan, China, and Korea come to terms that allow them to work together under Sudo's banner idea of "We are all one." Yet there's a looming spectre threatening the new peace, and oh look, he's obviously American.

As an American, I find it maddening that I have to look so far outside of my country to find out what people elsewhere think of it. I cannot, in mid 2014, deny their visions of the United States as a power hungry giant out for its own purposes. The overhanging vulture that is the USA cares little what happens in the world, so long as the results are beneficial to the USA.

Looking deeper at World Order's choreography, I see another commentary, this time upon the world of business. I do not think it accidental that World Order portrays businessmen moving in lockstep and in a robotic fashion. Returning for a moment to the stage of international governance, business and legislation are so cozy together that they no longer see any need to hide the relationship. Corporations rule the world, yet another foundation of cyberpunk fiction and the circumstances we inhabit today. The robotic nature and passive expression of World Order's suits and ties parodies the corporate world with its three piece suits and unfeeling outlook.

If you watch anime or Japanese pop cinema, you'll notice a recurring disaster, something relatively absent from American cinema. Japan has this nasty habit of getting destroyed. There are deep, psychocultural reasons for this but at its heart, Japan is as yet the only nation in the world to have a nuclear weapon used against it in anger. So it's not accidental that the methods of destruction revolve around the unleashed power of the atom. Whether it be a bomb or unintended consequences of nuclear radiation, like *kaiju* monsters and *Gojira* (Godzilla), the threat and effects of nuclear disaster is prominent with Japanese pop culture.

Yet Japan arose from the ashes of Hiroshima

and Nagasaki and this too is a common theme in anime and cinema. Neo-Tokyo — a newer, larger metropolitan Tokyo — is often literally built upon the ruins of Tokyo. Depending on the storyline and setting, it's possible that the two intersect and characters explore the ruins of old Tokyo. This characteristic flows through cyberpunk too, most notably in the seminal cyberpunk anime *Akira.*

In an unexpected parallel, World Order finds itself in similar circumstances. Machine Civilization is their biggest hit to date and it was produced just after the 2011 Tohoku Earthquake and the resulting tsunami. Unfortunately the Fukushima Daiichi nuclear power station was directly in the path of the oncoming tsunami and the consequence was another real-life atomic disaster for the island nation. As Japan struggled, and continues to to rebuild, Sudo created the song to encourage people to work together, to change in a positive manner. He writes on the music video's YouTube page:

The world is not going to change. Each one of us

will change. And if we do, then yes, the world will be changed. It is darkest right before the dawn. Let's all rise up to welcome the morning that will be so very bright for mankind.

The sentiment is echoed in the lyrics:

kono sekai wa kawareru no ka (Will this world be able to change?)
kono omoi wa maboroshi ka (Are these thoughts illusion?)

Deep within the plotlines of cyberpunk, there is rebellion. Of course there is, that's the punk part of cyberpunk. That rebellion is there because hope exists. People who deride cyberpunk for its darkness fail to see its light, because at the core of the genre there is a belief that the system can be fought and things can be better. The Buddhist ideal of "We are all one" may seem foreign to the cyberpunk outsider, but its an intrinsic part of the story. "No matter where you are… everyone is always connected," says Iwakura Lain, the title character of Serial Experiments Lain. Artificial

Intelligence constructs like Wintermute/ Neuromancer or the Puppet Master of Ghost in the Shell are quite literally born from the interconnectedness, the "oneness" of all things.

Cyberpunk references and ramblings aside, World Order is definitely worth checking out. Even if you don't speak Japanese there's a playfulness in their music that makes it fun, regardless of a language barrier. It's the age of the Internet so translations and lyrics are a search engine away. We are, after all, interconnected.

About the author…

Daniel Messer has worked in libraries for over twenty years, recorded podcasts for over a decade, wrote a few books, and still has no idea how to write something about himself. But people expect to see these kinds of things at the back of the book, so he'll likely tell you something about how he's the creator and host of the *Cyberpunk Librarian* podcast. It's a show that explores the intersection of libraries and technology with a focus on free and open source software.

Dan lives in Mesa, Arizona where it's usually warm, often hot, and sometimes hotter than hot. He listens to a lot of ambient and space music and partakes of far too much Irish folk music, especially when he's had a couple of bottles of Irish red ale.

Then again, that's when he typically thinks up these hair-brained ideas, so it works out in the end.

* * *

You can find his other books on Amazon, and you can tune in to Cyberpunk Librarian at:

https://cyberpunklibrarian.com/

www.ingramcontent.com/pod-product-compliance
Lightning Source LLC
Chambersburg PA
CBHW031225050326
40689CB00009B/1476

* 9 7 8 1 0 9 1 1 0 4 3 3 4 *